RULE
Your Own
ROOST

J.D. Sisera

Copyright © 2024 Independently Published

All rights reserved. No part of this book may be reproduced or used in any manner without written permission of the copyright owner except for the use of quotations in a book review.

First paperback edition July 2024

ISBN 979-8-3285-1488-0

For each one of you
who has ever dared to think
that maybe, just maybe,
you could...
AND SO YOU DID.

Contents

* * * * * * *

Walking on Eggshells?
(Author's Note)

#1 Nest Egg
(Your Biggest Investment - The Coop)

#2 Not All it's Cracked Up to Be
(Why Free Range is Not for Everyone)

#3 Don't Fly the Coop
(Chicken Run Ideas)

#4 Chicken Little or Mother Hen?
(Why You Might Start with Chicks Instead of Chickens)

#5 Time to Count Your Chickens
(Purchasing Chicks: When, Where, How Many & Which Kind?)

#6 Spring Chickens
(Preparing & Caring for Your Day-Old Chicks)

#7 Chicken Scratch
(Food, Water, Treats & Cheaps)

#8 Pecking Order, Ruffled Feathers & Fowl Play
(Can't We All Just Get Along?)

#9 First the Chickens, Now the Eggs!
(What To Do With All Those Eggs)

Don't Chicken Out!
(You. Can. Do. This.)

Walking on Eggshells?
(Author's Note)

A few years ago, I bought a house just outside of town....and it came with six chickens. The previous owner was not keeping them and offered them to me. I had no idea what I was getting into, so I'm still not sure why I said yes without any hesitation. I think it had something to do with idealistic visions and warm fuzzy feelings of farm-fresh eggs and simple country living. And while I wasn't wrong, I also wasn't ready!

I almost immediately regretted my decision. I had a coop and some feed, but I Didn't. Know. What. I. Didn't. Know - such as the implications of free range farming or why four roosters is a bad idea...

Now you are wondering the same thing - are you really ready for this? If you don't have your chickens yet, or you just got them and it's not what you expected, this book is for you! Perhaps your questions include:

- What are the start-up costs? Ongoing expenses?
- How much time and effort will this take on a daily basis?
- Am I raising chickens for eggs, as pets, maybe both?
- What kind of chickens should I buy and how many?
- Do I have space for this? Am I even allowed to have chickens on my property?
- Do I have what it takes to raise chickens?

While I may have gotten off to a rough start myself, let me just say that **raising chickens is really not that hard!** It doesn't have to be expensive or complicated. The basic concepts in this book are things I learned along the way, usually the hard way, by trial and error. This book is not about living off the grid or mass production. This is a straightforward, no nonsense guide for regular busy people like us who just want to save time, avoid headaches, minimize costs, and enjoy the benefits of raising your own chickens. **Let's do this the easy way!**

You WILL have what it takes! Get ready for EGG-ceptional results (the easy way.)

- J.D. Sisera

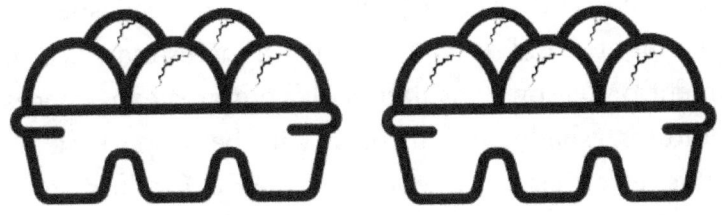

#1 Nest Egg
(Your Biggest Investment - The Coop)

First Things First
While you have likely already considered whether or not your property would be conducive to raising chickens, you should first check your local zoning ordinances or neighborhood bylaws. Find out if you are allowed to keep chickens on your property and if there are regulations about how many you can have at one time. Knowing this in advance can save you a lot of time and money if you are facing certain restrictions.

The Coop
Will you build your coop or just buy one? Consider materials you may already have on hand or an existing structure that could be repurposed. You may be able to save money by sectioning off some space in a larger building or altering a small shed. If you are only thinking about keeping a couple of chickens, save yourself the headache and just purchase a small, ready made coop from your nearest tractor supply store. Larger,

more elaborate coops are also available for a price, but they will save you a lot of time if you just want to get this step over with.

Consider the location of your coop, which also depends on the climate where you live. All chickens will need shelter from direct sunlight, wind, or rain. Colder climates may also require permanent or seasonal insulation. If your area experiences high temperatures, shade and airflow will be important. Easily accessible electricity will come in handy for box fans, heat lamps, or lighting in your larger coops.

Access to the Coop
Larger coops require a door large enough for you to enter the spaces needed. If your chickens will have regular access to outdoor space, they require a narrow ramp leading to a small opening with a latching door. Ready-made coops are generally designed this way and may have additional convenient features for accessing eggs or keeping the coop clean.

Nesting and Roosting
Chickens instinctively lay their eggs in small, contained, elevated spaces. If you do not provide a designated safe place for your hens to nest, you will find eggs laid in corners or nooks and crannies throughout their space. Ready-made nesting boxes can be purchased and attached to the interior walls of your coop. They should be filled with bedding, such as straw or wood shavings, which should be replaced frequently. You do not need a separate nesting box for each hen. More often than not, they will all lay their eggs in the same box! Almost any wooden crate or plastic box can be easily repurposed into a nesting box as long as it has a solid bottom and can be elevated off the floor.

Chickens generally feel safer when they are off the ground, which is why they also need a place to roost at night. Depending on the size and layout of your coop, this can be as simple as a narrow piece of wood or rod attached from wall to wall. While there is no reason to overcomplicate your coop with unnecessary decor, a simple and effective roost for a larger flock can easily be made by propping a wooden ladder against an inside wall of the coop. Just be sure there is nothing important beneath the roost - the space below it will quickly be covered with chicken droppings.

Keeping the Coop Clean
Speaking of chicken droppings, there will be a lot of it. A little proactive effort can save you a lot of time and help keep your chickens healthy. Both large and small coops benefit from an absorbent base layer, or bedding. Wood shavings, straw, or even mulched fall leaves are all viable options. Bedding is periodically removed from the coop along with the waste and replaced with fresh material. Ready-made coops often have some sort of removable pan or tray that can be easily emptied, which must be done frequently to avoid overflow. All nesting box bedding should be refreshed often as well. Larger coops using wood shavings on the ground will need to be shoveled at least bi-annually, which can be conveniently timed for use as early spring and late fall fertilizer if you happen to have a garden. Straw bedding or mulched leaves are more apt to mold or become soggy and will need to be refreshed more often. If you do not have a place to dump the waste, you may consider offering it to local farmers or gardeners. As an added benefit, they may also be willing to remove it for you!

Just for Fun
If your chickens will live inside the coop full time, you might add activities for them such as a swing made by hanging a dowel rod by two strings or a boredom-buster made out of a plastic

water bottle partially filled with small rocks. A dust bath, which will naturally repel fleas and parasites, is easy to create by laying an old tire on the floor of the coop and filling it with sand. Additional features can easily be added to your chicken coop at little to no cost. Just remember - everything in your coop will quickly be covered in chicken droppings...

#2 Not All it's Cracked Up to Be
(Why Free Range is Not for Everyone)

Location
The term 'Free Range' is typically used to describe chickens that are free to roam about wherever they want during the day. (Technically, this is called 'Pasture Raised.') If you live near a busy road or have neighbors nearby, allowing your chickens to roam freely is not your best option. Although chickens usually stay relatively close to their coops, they are very likely to trespass and will frequently wander into dangerous territory.

Predators
Imagine arriving home one day to find that your entire flock is completely gone, perhaps leaving only a few feathers of evidence behind to indicate the location of the crime scene. Chickens have a wide variety of natural and domesticated predators, from owls and hawks to your neighbor's dog. Your only defense options are unreliable scare tactics and a very protective rooster. However, a top-notch rooster will not take

kindly to people or pets either and you may soon find yourself wearing thick pants and close toed shoes every time you dare venture out into your own driveway. Hypothetically of course.

To Coop or Not to Coop

On most days, you simply open the door to the coop in the morning and your free range chickens will lazily wander out to enjoy the day. Most evenings, your chickens willingly return to the coop on their own at dusk and you will simply latch the door for nighttime security. But on some nights and for no apparent reason, your chickens will not return to the coop and you will spend unthinkable amounts of time trying to coax them out of your trees and bushes. They will be extremely uncooperative with your attempts to save their lives and it will likely start to rain while your neighbor watches out his window as you swat in vain at your flock with a broom. Hypothetically of course.

Feathers & Feces

Both of these things will be everywhere. Everywhere. Nothing says 'Welcome to My Home' like a front stoop covered in poop! Your chickens will be in your driveway and on your vehicles, on your patio furniture and even on your roof. While most chickens avoid nibbling on standard landscaping plants, your flowers will be in constant danger. If you have both chickens and a garden, at least one of them will need to be fenced in. Chickens will eat almost anything, but they especially love vegetables and will eat every. single. thing. in your garden. Hypothetically of course.

The Flip Side

While there are many challenges to raising free range chickens, it's only fair to acknowledge a few benefits so that you can make an informed decision. Free range chickens will do a wonderful job ridding their territory of bugs and small critters. Moles do not seem to like chickens and will avoid tunneling ground that is frequented by them. Free range chickens will add a fair amount of fertilizer and aeration to the lawn and will require significantly less purchased feed or supplements due to foraging naturally all day. But be forewarned; these potential benefits can be quickly offset by the many inconveniences and risks. These lessons are often learned the hard way. Hypothetically of course!

#3 Don't Fly the Coop
(Chicken Run Ideas)

Size Matters

Technically, the term 'Free Range' simply means that your chickens have the choice to be inside or outside during the day and that there is at least two square feet of outdoor space per chicken. If the contained outdoor space, called a chicken run, is large enough, then your chickens are still considered to be free range. Chickens will efficiently eat or scratch up nearly all plants or grass, which means the ground of a smaller run quickly becomes a combination of dirt and manure and can be muddy depending on the season and location. To determine the size of your chicken run, consider the cost of materials versus the benefits of more space. While fenced outdoor space is certainly not required for raising chickens, it is often preferred as a very happy medium between caged and pasture raised. Your chickens will benefit from fresh air, activity, and the opportunity to forage almost as much as you will appreciate factors such as convenience, cleanliness, and security.

To Cover or Not to Cover

Determine if your chicken run will be covered or not. As long as your chickens have continuous access to the coop, there is no need for a roof over the run itself. However, you should consider the availability of shade and security. Chickens can technically fly, just not very far. This is one of the reasons why you will either need to regularly clip their wings (no thank you) or determine a way to keep the chickens inside the run. The simplest and most cost effective way to accomplish this is to install mesh or wire netting over the top. Keep in mind that climbing or airborne predators will attack chickens even if they are fenced in, so a covering over the run prevents this issue as well.

Types of Runs

When considering which type of run to use, there are pros and cons to both permanent structures and movable fencing. As mentioned, your chickens will quickly dig up and eat every accessible plant. Smaller, movable runs are often cheaper and can offer your chickens a wider range of ground to forage. Long, narrow runs can even be placed between the rows in your garden to eliminate both weeds and insects. Regularly moving and stabilizing mobile runs, as well as returning your chickens to the coop at night, can be time consuming. The most common chicken runs are stationary runs. These can be expensive depending on the materials used, ranging from basic fencing to elaborate pergolas! However, once the run is established, there is little maintenance or effort required. One upgrade that will be worth every penny - choose hardware cloth or standard fencing over cheaper chicken wire. Many predators are able to tear through this flimsy material, so it should only be used as a covering, not for the perimeter of your run.

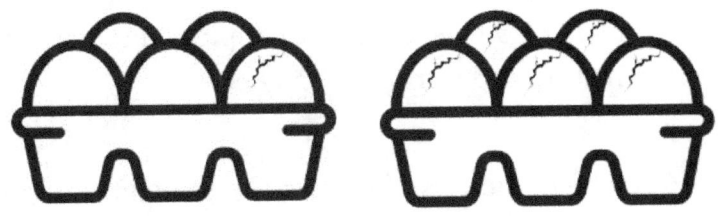

#4 Chicken Little or Mother Hen?
(Why You Might Start with Chicks Instead of Chickens)

Day-Old Chicks

There are three options when purchasing chickens with regards to age: baby chicks, pullets, or mature adults. The benefits to purchasing day-old, or baby chicks (up to 5 weeks of age), are that they are inexpensive, convenient to purchase at your local tractor supply store, and are easily imprinted. Holding the chicks and letting them see your face even a little bit every day causes them to imprint, or be comfortable around you. Adult chickens who have been comfortable in your presence since they were small are much more cooperative when it comes to feeding, collecting eggs, and even chasing down the occasional escape artist. This is especially important if you plan to raise your chickens as pets, but will make your life much easier even if you don't plan to spend a lot of time with them in the future.

Roosters and dominant hens are generally unfriendly, but those who are comfortable with their people are a lot less challenging to deal with! The main drawback to raising very young chicks is that they can be fragile; it is not uncommon to lose a few along the way. You will also have to wait a couple of months for your tiny hens to mature and start producing eggs.

Pullets

Pullets (6 weeks-12 months of age) can be thought of as teenage chickens. They are fairly hardy, no longer depend on heat lamps or special feed, and will soon be producing eggs if they aren't already. They can be more difficult and more expensive to obtain than day-old chicks, but can still be tamed with some effort.

Adult Chickens

Starting your flock with adult chickens may seem less risky, and it is true that your adult chickens are very likely to survive. However, it is nearly impossible to tame them and unlikely that they will ever feel comfortable around you even with effort. If adult chickens are your preference starting out, you will need to find a farmer who is willing to part with theirs as you cannot find adult chickens in a farm store. Beware the age of adult chickens; many breeds slow or stop laying eggs around 2-3 years of age.

Hatching Your Own Chicks

Attempting to hatch your own chicks is not recommended for people new to raising chickens, especially if you are still hoping to avoid headaches, lower costs, save time, and enjoy the benefits of raising our own chickens. But I'm sure it would be really fun to watch them hatch.

#5 Time to Count Your Chickens
(Purchasing Chicks: When, Where, How Many & Which Kind?)

Hens vs. Roosters
If you want eggs, you need hens, or female chickens. Many people are surprised to learn that a rooster is actually not necessary for egg production. However, if you hope to someday hatch your own chicks, a rooster is needed to fertilize the eggs. You may also want one rooster to help protect your flock from predators, especially if your chickens will be in an unsecured run or roaming around as they please. While you can freely add as many hens as you want, you will either want one rooster or zero roosters. Take note: more than one rooster is a bad idea, both for you and for the hens! When you shop for chicks, be sure to find out if you are getting sexed chicks (likely female) or straight-run (random mix). You may accidentally end up with several roosters and no fresh eggs at all!

Breed

There are so many breeds of chickens to choose from! Keep your goals in mind while making decisions here. Are you hoping for maximum egg production or are you more interested in raising chickens simply as a hobby or even as pets? Do you envision your flock having a certain look - either all the same or a diverse mix?

If egg production is your primary goal:
- Leghorn breeds are hands down your best bet. These prolific layers startle easily, but they are also hardy, easy to care for, and produce an average of 300 eggs per year - each!
- Rhode Island Reds also lay around 300 eggs per year, though they tend to have bossy personalities.
- If you are looking for a pet with benefits, consider ISA Brown or Buff Orpington, which are consistent layers but also very friendly.

All breeds mentioned so far are excellent producers and lay medium to large eggs. Leghorns have white feathers, while the others are light to medium brown and have the look of gentle mother hens as they sit on their eggs. As a general rule, white chickens lay white eggs and brown chickens lay brown eggs.

If you are looking for either unique eggs or standout feathers, there are many beautiful breeds to choose from:
- Ameraucanas lay blue eggs, and the Easter Egger breed can lay blue, green, cream, or even pink eggs! Both of these breeds have primarily bluish gray and brown feathers, sometimes with hints of iridescent blues and greens, and dark beaks and legs. And while these breeds are beautiful, they are not friendly.

- Barred Rock, Sussex, and Delaware are picturesque breeds with their combination black, white, or brown speckled feathers and will lay 2-3 eggs per week. Be aware that Sussex chickens can be quite noisy, making them less than ideal for suburban chicken keepers.
- Silkie chickens may be your top choice if you are simply looking for a pet. These birds have a fun and peculiar look with fluffy feathers even on their legs! They don't lay eggs often, but are great mothers if you are looking to hatch chicks. They are small and may get picked on by other breeds, but tend to be great with kids. Their quiet nature makes this breed a good option for small coops in suburban backyards.
- Bantams are another small, distinctive breed. These chickens are surprisingly petite, which means they take up less space and require less feed. Their eggs are quite small and vary in pale shades of white and cream.

There are many other breeds to choose from beyond what is mentioned here. However, these breeds are fairly easy to find and inexpensive to purchase as chicks. Mix and match your new flock however you like, keeping in mind that they may not always get along due to variations in size and temperament.

How Many is Too Many?

Consider your location and coop size. The number of backyard chickens raised in suburban areas may be legally limited to a specific number. If you purchase a premade coop, the packaging likely advertises a recommended flock size for the specific dimensions of the structure. Finally, determine how many chickens you really need if your number is not restricted. Raising chickens as a hobby or as pets requires only 1-3 chickens.

In order to harvest one dozen eggs per week, you will need 3-5 hens depending on the breed. Keep in mind that your hens will lay eggs less frequently during seasons with extreme temperatures or fewer daylight hours, so you may consider a slightly larger flock if this will be a concern for you.

When and Where to Purchase

Believe it or not, chicks can be ordered online in bulk. Local farmers can be another option when finding chicks for your new flock. Depending on where you live, the simplest place to purchase baby chicks is at your local tractor supply store when they are in season. Late winter to early spring is a great time to purchase chicks, but they will need to be kept warm when they are young. Because it takes 4-6 months for chicks to mature into adult egg layers, getting started with your chicks during the winter ensures they will be ready to lay when the weather is warm.

#6 Spring Chickens
(Preparing & Caring for Your Day-Old Chicks)

Home Sweet Home

Initially, your baby chicks will need very little space. If you have a small, movable coop, just temporarily bring it into your garage or weather-tight space until the chicks are old enough to move back outside.. A large bin or storage container will work just as well if it's at least 24 inches deep. If your coop is large or stationary, you could keep the chicks in a tub in the coop as long as they are contained and completely shielded from all types of weather. Spread a fluffy layer of wood chips or straw in the bottom of the tub, and you're all set! If you opted to move a small, bottomless coop indoors, save yourself a lot of hassle by first spreading a tarp or waterproof table cloth under the coop. Then spread a layer of bedding on top of the tarp for easy clean up later on.

Light

The amount of light your new chicks have is a lot less important than having a source of heat. A constant heat source, such as a heat lamp, is imperative for the survival of your day-old chicks. However, be sure the chicks can also move to an unheated space if they get too hot. It is not uncommon at this stage to lose a little one in the first few days, often because they are not able to regulate their body temperature.

Water

Another fatal danger to your chicks is their access to water. Fresh water needs to be available to them at all times, but the 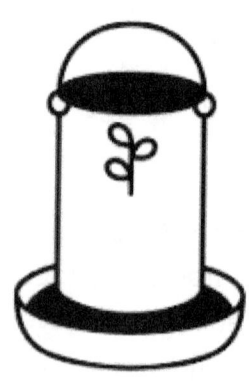 potential for the littlest chicks to drown is a very real concern. Farm supply stores carry a variety of options for this, similar to the one pictured here, which is convenient because it doesn't need to be refilled as often. Even so, the head of a tiny, topheavy chick can fall into the water and become trapped. One way to avoid this is to fill the rim with small rocks, which will allow just enough drinking water to be exposed. Any shallow container can be a suitable cost-efficient option, such as the lid of a peanut butter jar or a small bowl. Regardless of the type of waterer you choose, fill it with small rocks to alleviate risk.

Feed

Feed is the easiest part of caring for day-old chicks. Simply purchase a bag of chick feed, which will look like crumbs. Healthy chicks will not overeat, so just keep a steady supply. A large bag of feed will last a long time and is suitable for adult chickens as well so that you can use it up later as needed. As with waterers, there are also several types of feeders to choose from, or you can use something you already have on hand. Your chicks will quickly dirty or scatter anything they can walk on, so consider this when choosing a feeder.

Crusty Butt

Here's a fun one for you! At least a few of your chicks will end up with a clump of dried poo stuck to their bottoms. This must be removed promptly or the chick will not survive. Be sure to check the chicks daily for crusty butt (which is likely not the technical term!) Thankfully, this issue is easily resolved with a warm, damp paper towel - a little rub will take it right off.

Homecoming

Bringing your very first chicks home can be so exciting. You have prepared a space for them, carefully selected the breed you want, and now they are home! Likely, your chicks made the trip to your house in a small cardboard box. To ease the transition into their new space, just open and place the small box on its side near the heat lamp. They will come out when they are ready. Some chicks will stay in their original box for several hours, which is fine and will lessen the amount of shock they are experiencing. Once all of the chicks are roaming around, the box can be removed and discarded. You may eventually need to show your hesitant chicks where to find the food and water if they're too shy to go exploring on their own.

When Things Don't Work Out

Your new chicks will be quite fragile for the first 48 hours. Again, it is possible that a few won't make it. This doesn't necessarily mean you did anything wrong, or that you could've prevented it somehow. Assess the situation for potential improvements, but likely the chick was simply not going to survive for reasons outside your control. After the first few days, and especially after a full week, you will notice your chicks quickly growing and thriving! Within 7-10 days, the hazards mentioned in this section will no longer apply, and you will simply maintain your young flock until they outgrow their container or the weather allows you to move them to an outdoor coop. Change out their bedding, refill their food and water, and spend a few moments each day holding and coddling your brood!

#7 Chicken Scratch

(Food, Water, Treats & Cheaps)

Feed

Feeding your chickens is really just incredibly easy. They will eat (almost) anything. Even if your chickens spend the day foraging and don't eat much purchased feed during the warmer months, they will still benefit year-round from the protein and minerals needed for egg production. Many stores carry chicken feed and you'll get the best deals if you buy in bulk. As long as the food is stored in a very dry place, it will last forever. Use up any leftover *crumbles* that didn't get eaten by the baby chicks, but then switch to *pellets*. While they are both perfectly healthy for your chickens, the pellets tend to hold up better if they get scattered around in the dirt or bedding. Choose a feeder that will not allow your chickens to walk on the feed as it

will quickly be dirtied, scattered, and wasted. Raising the feeder off the ground a few inches helps as well; just stack a few bricks or pieces of wood to make a level, sturdy platform. Some models can also be attached to a wall. Large feeders and waterers will give you the freedom to leave for the weekend without worry.

Water

Chickens thrive with constant access to fresh water. A *hanging bucket with no-drip cups* or nipples will keep you from having  to clean and refill the water as often. Consider placing a few bricks under the basket, which will serve as steps for the shorter chickens and will also prevent the ground below the waterer from getting muddy. If you opt to use a shallow, open container, it will need to be rinsed out at least once per day. Any cheap or discarded container will work for feed and water, but to save time and headaches, top-load hanging water buckets are where it's at! The ones pictured are for larger coops, though similar smaller versions are available as well.

Calcium & Grit

Did you know that chickens eat rocks? Sand, grit, or tiny gravel is necessary for proper digestion. If your chickens have room to run outside, just toss in some grit material from time to time if they don't already have a place to find it on their own. Egg-laying chickens also need calcium in order to form eggs. A common store-bought source comes in the form of crushed oyster shells, but simply feeding all of your eggshells back to your chickens works just as well. (Chickens will eat their own eggshells?! Yep. They also like scrambled eggs and chicken nuggets.)

Treats

Occasionally, you might treat your chickens to sunflower seeds, mixed bird seed, cracked corn or corn cobs, or even suet blocks. These items can be readily found at a variety of stores, as can dried mealworms, which provide your flock with a boost of protein. When the weather is warm, surprise your hens with giant popsicles by freezing a bowl filled with food scraps or seeds and water. Hanging solid fruits and vegetables by a string or wire gives your chickens an edible pinata to enjoy. Dandelions or other weeds are a flock favorite. They love to scratch and forage around in large piles of rubbish, from food scraps to yard waste, and will be entertained by this for hours. Sweet treats, such as cookies or cake, are not harmful to your chickens, but are also not preferred by them.

Hazardous Foods

There are only a few seemingly random things that your chickens should not eat: raw potatoes or potato peels, apple seeds, onions, and rhubarb leaves to name a few. Learning the list of food hazards may seem daunting, but healthy chickens will refuse to eat these things anyway. You are free to give all food scraps to your chickens with reasonable certainty that they will be able to sort through it for themselves.

Chicken Food Cheap

Knowing the wide variety of food options your chickens will appreciate, there are many opportunities for free food. As mentioned above, your chickens will benefit from crushed egg shells, food scraps, weeds, perennial clippings or yard waste. If you also happen to have a garden, simply toss all rotten produce and old plants right over to your grateful chickens. Local gardeners of farm markets may let you take old or unusable produce at little to no cost. Excess pumpkins or winter squash, which you can obtain from a nearby corn maze or pumpkin patch, can be stored for quite some time and will allow your chickens to enjoy fresh food well into the winter. If your chickens have an outdoor run, you won't want to plant anything inside the coop because the chickens will quickly dig it up and devour it. However, you can plant flowers, bushes, or even produce around the outside. While a chicken may nibble at a plant through the fencing, it won't be able to get at the whole thing. This not only provides your flock with free food, but also adds shade and charm to your layout.

#8 Pecking Order, Ruffled Feathers & Fowl Play

(Can't We All Just Get Along?)

Danger from the Outside

Once predators have figured out how to break into your coop or chicken run, there will be an ongoing struggle until your defenses have been reinforced. First, determine how the predators are getting in. If they are climbing over the run, add a chicken wire or thick netting over the top. If the intruders are digging under walls or fences, dig 24" down along the perimeter and extend the fencing down into the ground. You can also line the outside perimeter with large rocks or bricks to deter diggers. Crafty egg thieves can even figure out simple door latches, which may need to be improved or doubled. Consider placing a closure at the top of the door and at the bottom. And finally, if a large predator, such as a dog, simply forced or chewed its way through the wire or netting, you can either replace it with thicker material, or eliminate the attacker and patch the holes with original material.

Danger on the Inside

Your flock will determine a definitive pecking order early on. The rooster will be dominant, but specific hens will emerge as second and third in command. Even with no rooster, the hens will still create a hierarchy with clear leaders. There will be a squabble any time members attempt to jump rank. This is the number one reason why having more than one rooster is a bad idea. While multiple roosters may occasionally fight each other, it is more likely that they will establish dominance by intimidating the hens through harassment and physical force. While all of this drama will likely be quite loud, you will also notice evidence of dissension when your hens begin to show bald patches where feathers have been ripped out during the attacks. Aggressors will also pluck out pieces of their victims' combs. The health of a hen's comb is a clear indicator of her egg production status. When the combs suffer, you can be sure the hens are suffering too. Rid your flock of the unwelcome roosters.

Newcomers also create opportunities for conflict. A mixed-breed flock with varying sizes and temperaments may struggle to agree on the status of each member. Adding new chicks to an established flock will throw your chickens into a state of chaos until a new order is established. Take care when introducing new chickens to your flock. Ensure that the newcomers are large enough and quick enough to evade attacks. Consider easing into the process by allowing only a short amount of time together at first and increase based on how well they are getting along. Consider adding a second feeder so they don't have to share right away. Don't rush it, or the newbies will not survive.

Sometimes chickens become disgruntled because they are bored. Toss in a new pile of weeds or lawn clippings, which will distract them for days at a time. Consider adding new elements to the coop, such as a stump or a thick branch to climb on, new bedding to forage through, or cheap boredom-busters as previously mentioned. Rest assured that whatever is causing the uproar will eventually work itself out, especially if you eliminate the primary culprit.

#9 First the Chickens, Now the Eggs!

(What To Do With All Those Eggs)

Gather the Eggs

Eggs are generally gathered daily. During seasons with cool temperatures, the eggs can remain in the nest for a few days as long as no rooster has fertilized them. Be especially prompt in collecting the eggs during very hot or very cold weather, as the eggs either start to develop or become frozen in extreme temperatures. Such eggs, along with any that are cracked, should not be eaten - by humans. Break those unusable eggs and let your hens reclaim all of that protein and calcium!

To Wash or Not to Wash

Your visions of pristine piles of glorious eggs sitting perfectly stacked in the nest just waiting for you to collect them? That is not real life. Unless you manage to grab those eggs fresh out of the chicken, they will likely be dirty with the same material that covers everything else in your coop! Most people choose to wash the eggs and store them in the refrigerator just like they would with store bought eggs. However, fresh eggs don't need to be refrigerated - unless you wash them. Unwashed eggs have a natural protective layer that keeps them from spoiling for several days. This can be reassuring if you aren't able to collect, wash, and store daily.

Quirks of Collecting

Do you know the egg-laying song? As your hens begin to lay regularly, you may start to notice a lot of commotion coming from the coop around the same time each day, usually late morning. One may never know whether the songs of your hens are inspired by the joy of delivering yet another egg or from the corresponding discomfort, but either way, the girls will tell you it's time with a reliable egg-laying melody.

Hens not laying?

The most common cause is lack of nutrients. Your hens must have enough water, protein, and calcium to produce eggs. Another cause may be lack of daylight. Because hens are hardwired to lay during longer, warmer days, you may need to add a light or bright heat lamp on a timer to the coop to ensure your hens receive at least 12-14 hours of artificial daylight during the winter. Note that heat lamps with red lighting are not bright enough to emulate sunlight. Even so, you can expect your hens to produce about half of what they would in the summer.

Age can also be the reason behind a lack of eggs. Most hens must be at least 16-20 weeks old to begin laying and a little older to reach full production. On the other side of the age spectrum, you can expect only 2-3 solid years out of your most prolific layers. After that, they will either become your pets or they will need to move on.

Disappearing eggs?

If you thought your hens were laying eggs but now you can't find any eggs, they are either being swiped by a predator, or your chickens are laying them outside the nest. If the latter is the case, try placing a fake egg or golf ball in the nest, which will remind your hens where they are supposed to be laying their eggs.

Mom won't move off the eggs?

Occasionally, a mother hen will become broody and not want you to get near her eggs. She may be stubborn, but she will be all squawk and no bite. You can pick her up and move her to the side with your hands if you feel comfortable, or shoo her out with a broom.

Too many eggs?

What a proud moment when your hens are laying faster than you can use up the eggs! Share your good fortune with neighbors, coworkers, or local food banks. Just know that your recipients will prefer you to wash the eggs first. You may even consider selling the eggs if you consistently have excess. Be sure to check your local or state laws first. Selling a few dozen now and then to people you know is usually fine, but if you start providing eggs to a farmers market or selling for consistent income, you may need a license and regulated package labeling. The process for this is not difficult or expensive.

And that's how you go from happy chicks to farm-fresh eggs!

You've put in the work; now you can really start to enjoy the fruits of your labor.

Don't Chicken Out!
(You. Can. Do. This.)

You got this. I promise. And when you don't got it... you'll at least likely end up with a funny story. The chicks, the chickens, and the eggs are great - that's the goal, right? But looking back, you'll also find you ended up with more than just eggs in your basket - you got an adventure as well.

I hope you found this book to be useful, encouraging, and possibly even a bit entertaining. If you liked what you read, please leave a favorable review on Amazon.com or on the site where you purchased this book. **I'm cheering for you!**

- J.D. Sisera

(References)

Certified Humane. (n.d.). *Humane Farm Animal Care of the Certified Humane Program*. Retrieved January 28, 2024, from https://certifiedhumane.org/

Chicken coach. (n.d.). *Chicken Coach*. https://chickencoach.com/

Home - American Egg Board. (2020, July 30). American Egg Board. https://www.incredibleegg.org/

Indiana State Department of Agriculture [https://www.in.gov/isda/]. (1 C.E.). *Home Based Vendors Frequently Asked Questions PDF*. https://www.in.gov/isda. Retrieved January 28, 2024, from https://www.in.gov/isda/files/Home-Based-Vendors-Doc-UPDATED-2.20.23.pdf

O, R. (2021, October 6). *Silkie Chickens | Ultimate Guide*. Mile Four. https://milefour.com/blogs/learn/silkie-chicken

Skyer, M. (2020, February 18). *10 most productive egg laying chickens*. Rural Sprout. https://www.ruralsprout.com/egg-laying-chickens/

Notes, Observations, and Adventures

FROM Your Very Own ROOST

You Did It!

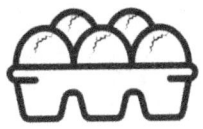

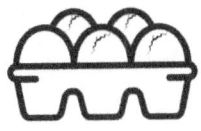

www.ingramcontent.com/pod-product-compliance
Lightning Source LLC
Chambersburg PA
CBHW070121230526
45472CB00004B/1364